# THE ENEMY WITHIN ME

# THE ENEMY WITHIN ME

## TRIBULATIONS COME AND GO BUT A
## CLEAN SPIRIT DEALS WITH IT SILENTLY

GASPAR ANDRADE

Order this book online at www.trafford.com
or email orders@trafford.com

Most Trafford titles are also available at major online book retailers.

Printed in the United States of America.

ISBN: 978-1-4669-4418-3 (sc)
ISBN: 978-1-4669-4417-6 (e)

*Trafford rev. 06/21/2012*

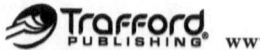 www.trafford.com

**North America & international**
toll-free: 1 888 232 4444 (USA & Canada)
phone: 250 383 6864 ♦ fax: 812 355 4082

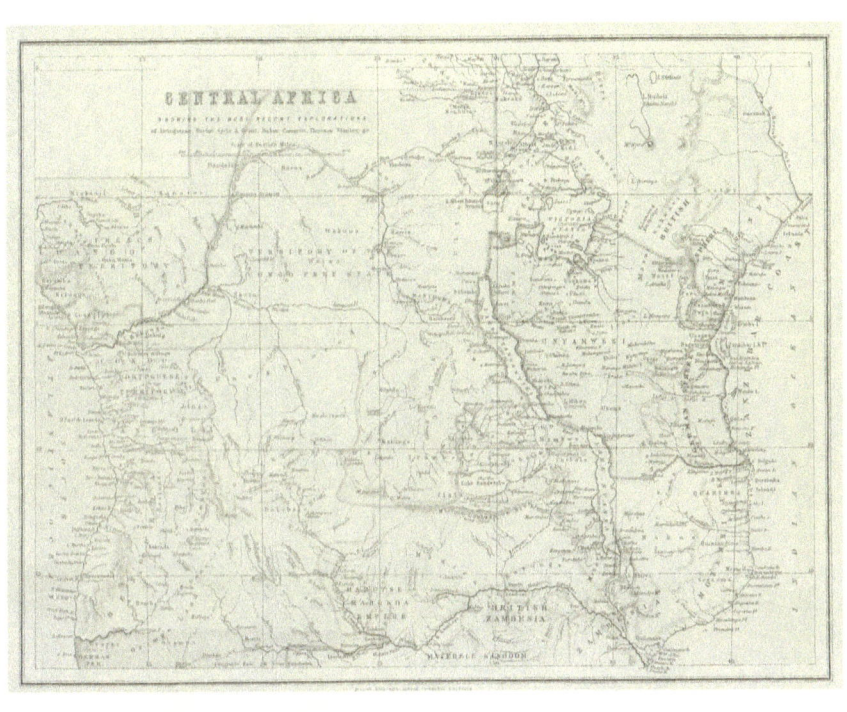

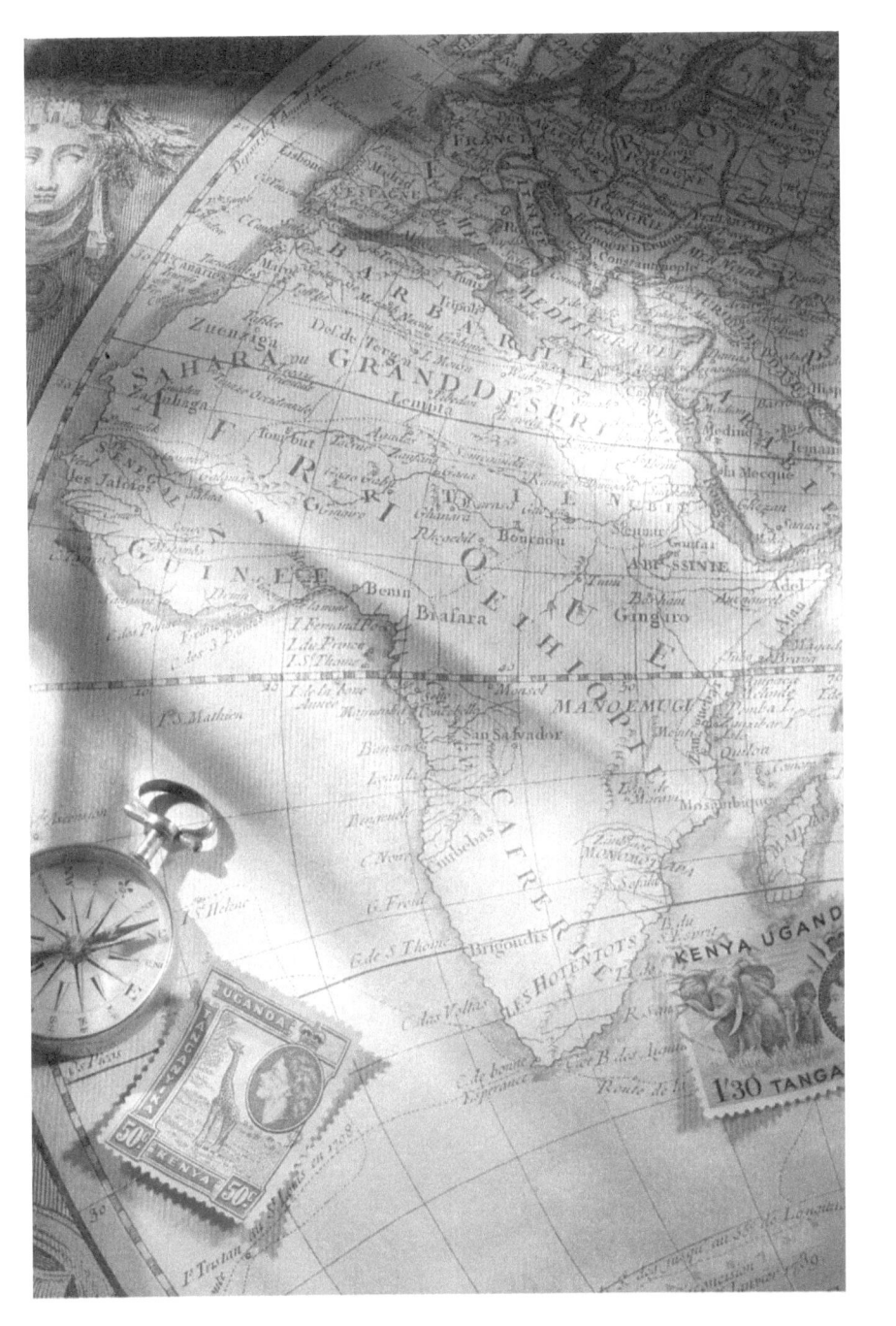

# CONTENTS

# PREFACE

My name is "GASPAR ANDRADE" and I am the author of this book. I was born in Angola, a southern country of Africa and in the southern coast of the Atlantic Ocean. A very warm and nice land filled with the beauties of Mother Nature. There is where Nature was born anyway and then expanded through the world. I wrote this book to let you get inside my world and feel my life as I take you to the journey of my true adventure. As human beings we all got lot in common than we really think. We are more connected than disconnected and we all feel the same things no matter the distance. It is like being unknown distant relatives in a mysterious place. As I take you to my journey, I want you to enjoy, feel, understand and envision your goals in life. The title of this book is "THE ENEMY WITHIN ME" and we are all enemies to ourselves. This book will help you see things differently. And make you pay attention to the little things that you thought meant nothing at all. To live is to suffer, to survive, to enjoy and understand the purpose of life. Life is for the livings, but sometimes the livings are dead and not knowing it. To appreciate the real you as you are, is a challenge for many. Well, tighten your seatbelts and let's travel to my world and experience my thoughts.

# MY BIRTH INTO THIS WORLD

I was born gifted in a mysterious life. Pretty much like being blessed and cursed at the same time in a world full of strife. People labeled me names and society always tried to force me to do things against my own will. So confused I started losing myself in this world and giving room to the unknown things to happen in my life.

The world is strange; yes it is a strange place. Full of mysteries and untold stories that shake our life. It's like the known living the unknown things and experiencing the incredible. The bitter sweetness that cannot satisfy the wishes and desires of the human being's flesh.

Being born in Angola–Africa, it was rough but it was nice. Africa is the cradle of humanity and the place where true things happen. Only in Africa you can feel and see the invisible and expect the unexpected. Memories run my emotions swiftly and softly to a magic place called dreams.

I was born to the most beautiful woman of my life. She is my one and only Queen on this earth. I call her Mama and she is my air that I need to breathe. Oh Mama, God bless you Mama.

Mama taught me the best things of this life. Yes, she did her best to raise me and my siblings in the best way she could. Mama did three beautiful things in my life that I will never forget. First she gave me birth, second she gave me education and the third thing she took me to church where I found God.

# MY MYSTERIOUS CHILDHOOD

We were seven people at home. "MAMA, my big sister PATRICIA, my big Brother SANTO-MANINO (R.I.P) I love you and I will always miss you big Brother, my other sister LOLA, then other sister ANINHA, my nephew CARECA and I". We were all from Mama's side and from Daddy's side; well I don't know how many siblings I got. And there we were, innocent ones exposed to a life full of Drama.

As a little man I never liked to surrender. Mama always said she loved me, but I was too shy or even too ashamed to say I love you too, Mama. A Single Mother working harder to raise her kids the right way. I used to tell Mama that I would make her life better when I grow older but always shy to let my feelings out about how I really loved her.

Mama can cook. Yeah Mama is the best and my role model. She cooks so well that makes you scream of joy when you eat her food.

Soul food is the kind of food that heals your heart and spirit when you felt broken.

Full of love, full of respect, full of courage, that is Mama. Strong belief in "JESUS", always proud of what she had even when things went wrong she stood firm like a soldier. I got my motivation and faith from Mama because she was always sure of what she did. Even when life could force her to kneel down, Mama always got up and moved forward.

In the poverty she raised us although our country is wealthy. The wealth was only serving the government and its family. Sometimes we had nothing to eat, drink or to wear. But Mama kept on doing her best to survive along with us her children.

In my early age; I realized that the real wealth of this earth wasn't the oil. It wasn't the diamonds, gold or silver. Neither was any other kind of resource that human beings die for to get it. But it was always the mindset along with the gifts in it.

People still don't know how wealthy they are. Those who know it, keep the others with depression in order to stop them from finding their real wealth. If we all had the same rights and see the truth, then there would never be downfalls. The ambitions to obtain much more from the other people's abilities and strength grow higher and maintain solid than ever.

# THE DRAMA
# WITH MY FATHER

My Father, well we never got along really. My Dad had lot of wives and he had money. He was never around and I had no feelings for him. I used to steal money from him when I used to visit him in his restaurant and he used to beat the crap out of me badly.

My neighbors knew who my dad was. A big man with big money but couldn't take care of his responsibilities. When he felt like visiting us then he would send one of his workers to check us at home. At the early age I began to feel the real meaning of being disrespectful and treated like garbage.

Eighty percent of the crimes in the world happen because of lack of fathers in the house. Fathers are father figures and when there are no father figures then the children lose themselves. Children need directions and guidance from fathers. Mothers are goddess but fathers are gods.

I had to learn and experience things the hard way. No direction at all and I felt like inside a dark tunnel for years. From that point of view I created my own motto that kept me strong when I was weak. And my slogan was, is and will always be: WHATEVER HAPPENS, LET IT HAPPENS BECAUSE I'M ALREADY IN HEAVEN: it kept me alive, well-motivated and stronger.

In the puberty of my life, my mistakes were my teachers. Abandoned and angry, I decided to force my father to see his own mess of not being around. I didn't want him to live with me if he didn't want to; I just needed him to be there for me as a real man. I used to humiliate him by stealing his money and everything I thought could hurt him.

Everybody in my family and neighborhood knew about my drama but I didn't care. The more my Father beat me, the worst things I could do to hurt him. In my mind I though, it was better for him to kill me then to keep on living without a Father. In a period of time he felt ashamed and began to pay a little bit of attention to us as his seeds.

I forced him to turn his neck on us and to see his mess. He began to support us financially for a while. It wasn't much although he could do more but it was nice and I felt alleviated. After a while he changed his mind again.

He used to send us money monthly and then there was a time he could send when he felt like. Going back to the same old spot, there I was once again. The little hopes of my life switched off again and it all got worse. Man, my Father was a Pimp; he had four to five families and a bunch of girlfriends.

But he had money to cover all his responsibilities and assume his position. I was never naïve to have him by us only and leave the other families. He was the one who left us, especially we as his first born. When you have many children, it is my belief that you deal with the consequences.

If you don't solve your problems, your problems will solve you. People keep on making the same mistakes, although knowing the outcome. It is easier to live with one hundred pigs then to live with a stubborn. So my life was miserable and my Father couldn't make us feel like family.

Humiliated and abandoned I used to feel when I saw kids in my age with their Father playing. The worse is my Father was his own boss and his company was one hour from where I lived. Every day he could go to his office, passing through the main road that went through our house and not coming to say hello. I used to cry like a baby inside and outside myself.

I used to be drunk in the pain and living in the anger of my life. I've been Powerless and drowned in the sorrow for years. Well, Mama always used to say: don't worry because God sees everything. My Mama and Father had some issues but for him to leave us like that, it was not right.

Dad used to beat Mama so bad that it affected my mind. One day he came to our house and snatched one of my sister and me and took us to his house where he lived with his other family, my half siblings. As we got there, he beat us so badly that it made me hate him. Until today I don't know why he beat us that bad.

In front of my half siblings and my step mother he was trying to prove a point perhaps. It was terrible, horrible and just insane. Living under my Father's roof was like living under a dictator with the love never dwelling in there. I know very well the definition of pain and oppression.

I know what it is like being a captive. In the prisons of the governments are bad. But in the prisons of injustice made by your own blood are worse than anything else. Taking me from my Mama by force it broke my world completely.

I never wanted to leave my Mama and if I could, it had to be my own decision. Although I was taken from my Mama by force, but Mama was never taken from me. In my heart, soul and spirit there was my Mama and I could hear, feel and sense her from faraway. My Mama is a beautiful black woman and in me I could hear her soft voice and see her lovely eyes looking at me.

In my dreams Mama used to tell me be strong and keep God always above all. Every time I asked my Father to go and visit my Mama, he would scream at me with a crazy attitude. So I had no other choice but to escape from there with my sister and going back to live with my Mama. My Father was angry as hell and went to pick us up and took us back to his house.

The more he could beat us; it wasn't really worthy because we would escape again and go back to Mama. It became like a crazy game that would repeat itself over and over and over again. He would pick us up and take us to his house and we would escape every time. I used to run away from my Father's house because I wasn't used to the life he had.

I love my half siblings for sure but I couldn't live in their environment. I was raised by Mama and my spirit was next to her. Around Mama I had Love and around my Father I had hate. I learnt that when couples got issues and they got children, learn how to separate their issues from their children.

The results of arguments from parents affect children so bad and damage their future. Parents should talk to their children and be specific and willing to do what's right to keep them happy. Most of the problems we got in our society are because of bad parenting. I swore to God never raising my children the way I was raised.

My Dad's influence was nothing but a mess in my life. Parents should be friends with their children. And when the opposite happens, Lord knows how ugly that can be. Lot of children are what they have become today because of bad parenting.

Most of them would be great men and women in this world, but their parents stole their childhood from them. Let the children be children and enjoy the beauties of life. When you raise a child right, even if he or she does something wrong but they will overcome it with love and wisdom. Every human being was blessed with gifts and abilities to succeed in life.

But the devil always uses someone close to them to deactivate the blessings within them. It is a war to move from deactivation to activation. And only few people win this fight because most people fight against the wrong enemy. So there are winners, there are losers and there are neutrals.

# MY STREET LIFE

Winners are those who fall and get back up again. Losers are those who give up before things even start. Neutrals are those living and not knowing anything at all. So growing up in the ghetto, I tried to be somebody that was never me.

Just like everyone else, I thought it was cool. Around poverty and misery in my neighborhood things seemed so normal. I had nothing to lose, there I thought just like everyone else. I grew up around criminals and real bad people.

Bad men who loved to kill for fun and never cared about life at all. As a young man I thought my life would end up just like the lives of those I saw in my environment. Even though there were bad people, but we still had good people doing good works in our area. And the girls always told me I was cute and wanted to be around me.

I used to feel powerful and greater than Superman. Although we were broke, but the love was always within us and it was so true. It was from back then where I realized that there is something greater than money and anything else. Christmas in the ghetto was fabulous and full of love.

In other part of the world they celebrate it in the snow but we celebrated it in the summer. A great weather carried by the nice smell of Mother Nature. The neighborhoods decorated with palm trees on the entrance of every street and paintings on the walls that represented nothing but love and peace. It was cool though; yeah things were unexplainable.

It was really amazing. Tourists from all parts of the world used to come and see the nature we got in Africa. We were young and innocents living in a wonderful but sad part of this world. The gifts were there and given to one and other with enthusiasm.

But the things that were exciting were the events that the elders organized. A Great Culture full of nice Music being played for the crowd who loves love. Beautiful smiles in the sweet lips from nice people. Dancing competitions and being known by the people was greater than the price of winning the contest.

The ones who had fame had more power than the ones who had the money. Still they had to pay the events but the respect laid on those with fame. In a community of poverty, the love embraced the people and made them feel worthy. School was excellent, but I never really cared about that.

I was a great pupil growing up, but I used to ignore it. I started losing my great abilities to read and write because I was paying more attention to the streets. One day my Portuguese teacher asked me to read and I was so embarrassed that I started sweating as I read a book in the class room to a point where the book got wet of my sweat and the girls began to laugh at me. I was the strongest pupil of the school with low-grade.

I was the most well-known guy in my neighborhood around young guys, with a problem to read. The fastest runner and full of muscles, but with a confused mind. There I was, born blessed but selling my gifts so cheap to a lifestyle that only takes and destroys whatever it catches. And to make things worse, my country is a wealthy country but we were poor and living under terrible conditions.

# THE CORRUPTED
# GOVERNMENT OF
# ANGOLA

Angola is a very rich country with the potential and capacity to supply a greater life to all the Angolan citizens inside and outside the country. We are rich in Oil, diamonds, Coffee, Cotton, exotic animals and a great wild life given to us by Mother Nature. Unfortunately the population lives below poverty rate making it eighty to ninety percent of the whole population living under poverty. The ten percent is the government and they are the only ones who benefit from the riches of the land.

People die because of bad health problems and the pollutions are nothing new to everyone. Those with power drive expensive cars, have good lives and only walk with security guards to protect their possessions. People die like mosquitoes where I come from and the life condition gets only worse. The president is a dictator and the worse is; he is not a real Angolan citizen but run the country over thirty years with blood on his hands.

The police misuse their power as authorities and take advantage of the people. If you rise against them, they kill you because they are too cowards to see the truth. It is a rich country where the foreigners benefit from it much better than the citizens of the country. The people are tired of the dictator president and want him out forever but he threatens the people with death, imprisonment and punishment if the people revolt against his system.

The wealthy is the government alone and their slogan is blank everyone else as long as they got the power. They never cared about us and we never cared about them. The unfairness among the people was going on through the whole country. Young and old fighting for something that brings nothing but pain.

Caught up in the middle of that mess was hell and it was so hot that you could feel the heat burning your body. Despite of the love, the hatred was always trying to break loose at any cost and gain terrain. As people started to change they began to show their true faces. The Sons revolt against their Fathers and the violence was moving in silence.

The Fathers kill their own sons for the sake of money. The Daughters beat their own mothers. The mothers sleep with the husbands of their daughters. And more Fathers rape their own daughters.

The Parents sacrifice their own children for nonsense. Neighbors who were closed ones becoming strangers to one another. The rise of self-destruction was on the way with lot of evil works to do. Things were falling apart so unexpected and suddenly we were deep in the bitterness of life.

The friend within me told me that I was a champion, an overcomer, a good one and visionary. But the enemy within me told me that I was a loser, a bad guy and always showed me the reality of this life to prove me its point. So many Problems used to come unexpected and damage anything that I tried to build. Slowly but surely the invitation of death was around the corner of my joint. I was forced to be a man at the early age. Life was showing me the unfairness of it and I had to learn things fast. My childhood, well I don't really have a childhood. It was taken from me by the civil war and family issues that I had to face back home.

In the war zone, things happened like seasons. One minute we could be cool and the next minute we could act a fool. I still remember very well the criminals that used to destroy schools and cutting teachers breasts to leave their signs as evil ones. They used to call themselves (CAIXAO VAZIO) meaning (EMPTY COFFIN) in Portuguese. They raised hell in the neighborhoods and throughout the country. Oh boy, they were such a threat to our community. If anyone could have said their name joking while people were in the schools learning. Everybody would get out of their classes and start running with no directions like stunned birds.

Even the government couldn't catch them. They were like ghosts who appeared and disappeared at any time. Rumors were spread that they drove with coffins in their cars. Raping girls, stabbing and killing in such way that one could never imagine. As time changed, things got worse. The criminality became no longer silent and its voice was being heard loudly as the civil war was going on. No democracy at all and the corrupted government could kill and imprison anyone they would see or feel like getting them. So the civil war, the street war and family war; all of that was activating the enemy within me to perform bad things.

The rich got richer and the poor poorer. This philosophy wasn't new but applied to a younger generation. A generation born to be prospers but overshadowed by the ambitions of the older generation. The government killed us live and they felt no shame on doing that.

Many people got a good life, but not a happy life. They confuse themselves about it. Having a good life isn't having a happy life. But having a happy life is having a good life and much more. I always wondered how it felt like to be born rich. Living in the most beautiful places and having the most expensive houses in the nicest suburbs of this world. I wanted to feel and compare the conversations of rich kids and poor kids. I wanted to experience the sweetness of wealth.

Do ever rich kids feel hungry?, Do they get bored of life?, Do they know that it is a privilege to live their lives? These questions were mine trying to understand why some of us are rich and most of us are poor. Who am I? Why am I here? Where am I going to? And why do I exist? Why do I feel, smell and sense? Why do I look, envision and think? How can I dream, see and understand? Little questions but key questions of our lives and many don't know the answers.

Physically sleeping but spiritually travelling through the world. Seeing the unseen and hearing the unheard of this life. I was having the experience of living two lives in one world at the same time. Life is unexpected and unexplainable when the number nine turns to number six and the number six turns to number nine.

So many days and nights just were passing by and you flying inside your mind. The adventure of life that we all experience but only few can describe. Still the war between my Father and I got deeper. He wouldn't give up and neither I.

He changed many houses and took me along with him and my new family. Like before, every time I had the chance to escape, I did it. I've been through many different schools and neighborhoods. Faraway from Mama I was forced to move on.

Living bitter and sour inside myself. The outside of me was harder than stone and stronger than iron. Dad forced me to forget Mama. That was the biggest mistake he did to my life.

No matter what parents go through with each other, they should be able to explain to the children the reasons why. So that the children can understand and make their own decisions based on what happened between both parties. Dad never sat down with me and explained his point. Mama did and I saw with my own eyes what happened to her.

Instead of sitting and explain himself, Dad overthrew the principals of friendship between father and son. There is when things got out of hands opening doors for destruction. He had the power to control my social and financial life. But he didn't have the power to control my mind and soul.

Physically I was trapped under his roof for years. But spiritually I was free and wise enough to know that no matter how long it took, someday I would be grown in every aspects and he would never had to force me to do anything that I didn't want to. As I grew older I had the chance to travel. Seeing other countries of Africa and going to Europe.

# FROM AFRICA
# TO EUROPE

Dad thought he had brainwashed me that's why he paid those tickets for me to travel. He still wanted to control my life from overseas. I integrated myself to the European culture. Learning their languages and knowing more about them.

Germany, Holland and Belgium are the European countries where I made and left my true story. I learned a lot from them and they learned a lot from me too. Mutual respect and Cultures although the racism was trying to break loose. The time was well spent and the journey was really amazing. I've seen Historic monuments, great museums, and old cities with crazy true stories. I've been to great parties with no ends, enjoying life to the fullest, seeing things that make sense and nonsense at the same time. Life in Europe is much more expensive than life in Africa and it is a very developed continent with lot of bad secrecy. Things were not easy at the beginning but I made my way up and reached the top spot where I wanted to be as a foreigner.

# MY EXPERIENCES WITH LOT OF WOMEN

I started mingling myself with rich folks and trying to taste their lifestyle. The experience was shocking to me that it almost killed me. I started dating European women. I dated many wealthy women with power and good intentions.

I dated couple broke women too. But I was in a phase of feeling and enjoying my youth. A Lot of rich girls love to experience crazy things. I guess the money is too much that they feel boring so quick.

They love black guys like me and enjoy when you put it down correctly. But they are lonely, lonelier than the poor ghetto children. Loneliness is isolation, loneliness is sadness. Loneliness is having everything and not knowing what to do with it.

You can be with millions of people surrounding you and still be lonely inside. If your spirit is not happy then your life is not really worthy. Many of them hide themselves behind alcohol and drugs. It's a struggle to make it through the day without getting high or being under heavy influences of something.

Most rich people pay the highest price for that. Because they can get anything they want at any time, so the freedom becomes demise. I was in Expensive cars, expensive houses, expensive clothes and jewelries. I've tasted Exotic food, erotic mood, sympathetic smiles and the great competition among themselves.

Who got the best, which raise the most, which is doing more good to their community? But all that means nothing because when they go behind themselves they see and feel the reality of hell in their real life. My thoughts about rich kids grabbed me up. It was the opposite of what I've ever thought about.

Deep in their hearts something eats them alive. They die slowly watching themselves go off and not doing something about it. That's why many of them got bad manners, I guess. Many of them are mean and got no feelings.

They eat, take a shower and sleep worrying about their wealth. It's more like a nightmare than enjoying the enjoyable. I've been to some of the best restaurants and hotels of Germany, Belgium and Netherland. I've eaten some of the worse food in those places too.

Beautiful places and beautiful women were with me. But I wasn't really happy because my soul was burning. It's like living outside of you but dying inside. Enjoying the flesh and killing the soul at the same time.

Few people understand what it is like what I'm saying right here. Some people live in heaven and hell at the same time inside of their own bodies. It is rough, yes it's so tough. Going through life issues and not knowing what to do about it.

We think the evolution made us so civilized. But it takes nothing more than a natural disaster to see how primitive we still are. I had a rich lady that wanted to marry me so bad. She was fine and older than me ready to start her new life with me.

She was married before and didn't want to be with her husband any more. I was her first African man and she told me she never had somebody like me in her entire life. She was an Independent woman with two kids. Married to a wealthy man and they both had everything. Fifteen years with her man together. And her first fifteen days with me, she told me that her life with her husband was nothing but a lie. We had a good relationship, though. I enjoyed her as she enjoyed me very well.

I liked her but she loved me so much. There was the problem, I just wanted to have fun but she wanted more and I couldn't love her.

She bought me nice clothes and bling-bling. She used to buy me original stuff and very expensive ones.

She even wanted to live with me in Switzerland and start a new life with me there. Strange things happen in the world of money and if you are not prepared to see it, then you may lose your mind set. Before I met her, I used to roll with buses and trains. Then when I met her I used to ride on expensive cars of her.

I had no driver's license so she got a driver for me. That guy would take me anywhere I wanted to solve my issues. The dream of many but only few got to live it. In this life there were so many interesting conversations that were never spoken in Public.

The wishes and desires that never had the chance to come true. This life is full of ups and downs, ready for anybody at any time. My friends used to call me dumb because I left that woman. She was sexy and great but I wasn't feeling her the way she was feeling me.

Everybody told me I was stupid and I had to take all her money or most of her money then leave her or just stayed with her and pretended to love her. Well, it is easier to say when you are not in that position. I left the rich lady because spiritually we were not on the same path. I left her because she loved to control me so much in everything that I did.

She even wanted an account where the money would be in our both names if we could get married and live together. God told me not to do that because it would cost my life. Anything that you didn't work for and you get it is a curse. From your own sweat you shall enjoy the fruits of your labor.

Reap what you sow and live with it. A troubled soul attracts nothing but destruction everywhere it goes. When somebody trusts you with their wealth and you take advantage of them, you will see the results. When somebody trusts you with their life and you trick them up, you won't live happy.

When you manipulate people around you, then you are nothing but a punk. You think you are so cool, but you are just a fool. So many people are in prison, but mentally and spiritually free. So many people live out of prison, but mentally and spiritually jailed in their lives.

A man with issues is like a dirty toilet. If you don't clean it up, nobody is going to use it. People are like seasons. People change dramatically.

Everywhere I went, every people I met they all seemed so negative and aggressive. Life is hard; yes life is even harder when the positive isn't progressive. People live with secrets that eat their hearts alive. Some of them even choose to die with secrets that burn their souls forever.

Some lie and fake so much that they don't even see the difference between what's real and what's false no more. Just like the movie true lies from Arnold Schwarzenegger. When you have a dream, don't tell people about it. Some people are jealous of others and just love to destroy what's good.

I learnt to surround myself with people who know more than me. I love to lean more and move forward with a clear vision. If people think lesser than me then I move away. It's not that I don't love them; it's that their mentalities are contagious.

To be great, you must think great and be around the greatest. To live with freedom and wisdom I must go up and not down. When I left the rich lady, she cried like a baby. Asking me why and what was wrong with her that led me to leave her.

She almost killed herself and was hospitalized for a while. I got the chance to meet her husband and two kids and we had no drama. Her husband had other relationships too and she wanted to do the same. Both never believed in God and didn't want to.

She told me she couldn't be my normal friend because her feelings for me would never die and could lead to something crazy. So I decided to go my way and forget her forever. I found out that no matter how rich or poor a woman is they all just look for one thing in a man. Most of them are still confused and can't make up their mind.

Women got heavy self-issues and they so fragile. They can break any time at any place and go off forever. The one and only thing women look in to a man is "SECURITY". Most of them feel it but don't know what they are looking for.

No matter how rich or powerful a woman is in her life. But she stills a little beautiful girl deep in herself who is looking for the real security for her life. They look for Security as guidance and security as the physical and spiritual protection. They look for Security as the sexual comfort and security as the financial stability.

Security on her deep emotional issues, true father figure that can lead her and advise her to a certain point where she feels she can trust and it is worthy. I was the security of that rich lady and that's why she could trust me with her wealth and her deep secrets that even her husband didn't know. Everyone needs someone to love and to talk. Nobody can do everything on his or her own.

We all need each other even though sometimes we don't see it. In this journey of life called "DAVID VS GOLIATH" we are born full and have to die empty when we go home to the Lord. I went on living my life and discovering more issues that burned the inside of me. I've been Cruising in the spots of real racists and evil human beings.

# MODERN SLAVES
# IN AN OLD WORLD

I deeply believe as life rapes you, if you don't rescue yourself to move on positively, then you will get more evil than the devil himself. Some of us can change, but others will never ever change. In the belly of the beast so called devil's kitchen. I've been choked off by the evil deeds of devil sons.

I've been witnessing the field of unfairness and destructions. There I was caught up in a new chapter of the bitterness. I had a new kind of pain and a new kind of humiliation. I had a new kind of stress and a new kind of view.

I was facing a new kind of drama in a new area. But it all in the same old mind of mine. European government workers assigned to raise hell in public offices. You are already tired and stressed and they give you more stress every time you try to solve your public affairs.

The law that should be protecting civilians is nothing but a joke. Feels like living the end of our times and lives in here. Everybody stressed and depressed. The smiles and thoughts of good things had left us long time ago.

We are Young in age but old in the minds and souls. Pension nowadays is nothing more than crap for real workers who deserve real dignity and peace. I saw people dying at the age of twenty and being buried at the age of sixty. So many of them, good people with good hearts.

They have been trapped in the System that kills you mentally at the age of twenty and buries you when you are sixty years old. In that path of life; I was one of them but managed to get away. I was a Lion in the middle of hyenas. They were ready to kill me with no mercy in their eyes.

No matter if you are good to them, they will kill you anyway. The spirit of evil enjoys nothing more than doing evil things especially to those that are a threat to them in their environment. I remember working on a nine to five. I had a daily job with a cheap wage that ate me alive.

We start from Monday to Saturday, months and years on it. I used to call myself modern slave with an attitude of killing everybody at my job including myself. I had some Jobs. Silly jobs I did to keep me going where I wanted.

My friends once told me, if you could be with that rich lady you wouldn't be doing this Job. For a minute they were right, but the next minute I made the right decision. Still I used to feel sorry for myself. I used to work harder and harder for monthly crazy Cheque.

Modern slavery still exists and most of us don't see it. I know how it feels like to live in hell and knowing where you are. Back at the days the slaves knew that they were slaves and the fact that they couldn't do anything about it, they accepted it and lived with it. Nowadays we are slaves to the same system but we don't see it.

We are Working days and nights to feed our families and to survive. The worse is, not knowing that we all still slaves in a modern world that don't care about us. Every day working, we work so hard with no knowledge at all. No matter the weather conditions we just work.

Hating ourselves and hurting our hearts. Working from pay cheque to pay cheque and getting scared to be fired at the same time wanting to quit. Cold nights and sleepy eyes but you got to work. Not feeling well at all, still you got to work.

Asking God why do we live like this and then you will go to work. We sacrifice something so big to have something so small that we call it work. Work is great when it is worthy working. Working makes fun when you can earn a wage that put you in a position where you can help others too.

Nowadays employers and Employees are like Pimps and Prostitutes. They Pimp you up to a certain point where you kill yourself before you know it. It's all about the money. Not the Employees but the money.

As long as you are strong they will use you until you drop dead. They too don't care about us like the government. I still remember times in the early morning snowing, going to work on a bus and train so angry and frustrated. We all workers so pissed off looked like going to a funeral that never ends.

Sad faces, scared bodies, painful souls and gossip voices. That is hell on earth burning us alive. We go to work in the early morning still dark and coming home from work already dark. You don't see the daylight at all and gets worse when you work in a covered place.

Grown men but given only thirty minutes as break to eat something through the whole day. And most say that's normal, it's ok. Your debts are more than your wage. Every month you must work to pay the debts ahead of you.

If something extra comes your way, you can buy it because the money is already well planned. This is not life, it shouldn't be like that. I was born with talents but rejected because of racism. People didn't want to work with me because I was greater than them and some because of gender or bullying.

There is secret group of people with power who slowly and silently enforce evil things in our lives. They want to work on our mind set to make us obey them and fear them at any time. Every minute in our lives, somebody is born. And as somebody is born, somewhere in our lives somebody is killed.

A life comes and the other life goes out. Mysteriously things happen and nobody is safe anymore. I'm being followed and controlled like an animal in the zoo. We are being followed and controlled like animals in the zoo.

Inside our houses doing private things but they are watching us all. They know all our business and laugh at us as we perform them privately. Billions are spent for wars that we don't need. If love is the key, then why should I kill my brother for the sake of money?

We are all on planet earth but not on the same page. Just like the Hip hop artist Nas said: SOME OF US HAVE ANGELS AND SOME OF US HAVE DEMONS: In the darkness, friends are few. In the darkness relationship reduce to a certain point that makes you cry. In the darkness there is where you see who loves you and who don't.

To pass the test you must be willing to sacrifice and let something of your value die in order to get there. The Bible talks about sacrifices a lot. Real love is sacrifice although many don't know it. If you are not willing to sacrifice something, then it won't be worthy doing it.

Know what you do and do what you know with the blessings and wisdom of God. There are always two sides of things. There is Heaven and hell, Good and bad, Angels and demons; Sacrifices come also like this, the good sacrifices that in the beginning you will regret and then at the end enjoy. And there is the evil sacrifice that in the beginning you will enjoy and at the end regret forever.

# UNFAIRNESS OF LIFE

I've been judged by strangers and family members. I've been thrown under the bus for no reason. People that thought they knew me got me really disappointed. As 2PAC said: ONLY GOD CAN JUDGE ME: and in this life many people did me really wrong.

They were People that I loved with all my heart and soul. Some of them were my own family, friends and girlfriends. I wanted to die and if I had the chance to see them at that moment, then I surely could kill them too. I helped so many people overcoming the errors of their lives.

God knows all the good deeds I performed from the bottom of my heart. Things that I didn't have to do but I did it for the sake of passion and compassion. I used to cry loud and asking God why do people are like this. The more good things I did to people, they disappointed me badly.

Some of them were in the middle of death and I stood firm with them when no one else was there. People forget so fast the good things that you have done for them. But when it's negative, they remember so quickly. I decided to forgive them, yes I did.

# THE MINDSET
# IS THE TREASURE

I forgave them and moved on. It was never easy but I did it. Most of them I love them from faraway because it is better like this. Forgiveness is not an emotional issue but decision issue.

When you forgive you will still feel hurt and crazy. But as long as you decide to forgive, you really bless yourself. Because it takes an overcomer to forgive and an idiot to keep on dwelling in the same issues that happened longtime ago. Kings of this world are demons in hell.

Some walk, drive or travel with the best things of this life attracting the eyes of many to follow them and take them to hell. They even know the specific time and dates of their death because they made deals with devil. Sad but it's true and they smile like nothing is wrong with it. Governments are the solution to our problems, but they don't solve them.

Matter of fact they are willing to burn us and drive us insane. The news became nightmare and scares people to death. Entertainment is controlled by darkness and shows our minds how to obey the principals of madness. You, them and I on the same page dealing with the same oppressor.

We don't have a life but we have a nightmare playing with us. Things that you love, they force you to hate it. And things that you hate, they force you to love it otherwise they threat you with punishment and death. We were given the earth to protect it, but we destroy it.

We were given each other to live in harmony, but we kill one another. We are our best friend and worse enemy. When we judge each other, we just judge ourselves. If I don't need you then why do I live with you?

If we are brothers then why do we betray ourselves? If you love me then why do you hurt me so bad? We fall into our own trap and still wonder how that happened. I've seen people being burnt alive.

I've seen people being buried alive. Human beings and pigs flesh seem the same when they are burnt. The difference is on that taste and smell. So much Innocent blood fell on the ground like flood.

They didn't care because killing their own kind was their hobby. It was so hard to sleep every night. Whenever you hold a gun towards someone, your spirit automatically changes to something dark and evil. Murder, murder, murder and kill, kill, kill they shouted.

No mercy and no love in the faces of those who practiced evil deeds. A little thing could turn up to a big thing with blood in the hands. And they enjoyed it; yes I could see it in their faces. There is a War in the schools between teachers and students.

There is a War in the work between employers and employees. There is a War In the streets between good friends who knew themselves their whole lives. And war at home between family members. We all struggling and fighting for nonsense.

No trust, no passion and no feelings. Everything is upside down in our world. It should be something better but unfortunately the reality strikes where it hurts the most. If you could say something right, they could beat you to death or imprison you for a long time.

Some people until today never came out alive. The method of fear was put out to rule the society. Still we face it nowadays in most part of this world. We deal with Suppression, oppression, obsession and possession. We see Corruption, no emotion, manipulation, no authorization to a free nation.

We are oppressed and threaten every time we try to say the truth. Lost in the world but still with the hopes of BOB MARLEY and waiting for a: REDEMPTION SONG. Our mind is the battle field. Our mind is what they are after to capture.

The people are more valuable than the ruler. In this life the ruler is more valuable than the people. A king with no people is dead. A government with no people is done.

They are nothing without us, but they misuse us badly. If we were all equal, then we would live happily. God created us all equal Human beings. He made us all the same way and loved us all the same way too.

The capacity of each of us lay deep in ourselves. We all got the power that rose "JESUS CHRIST" from the dead, but they try to deceive us. A simple word can sweeten your day or embitter your day. A simple word can even heal your soul or kill your life.

# GOD IS THE
# ONLY SOLUTION

It is easier to do wrong and move from positive to negative. But it is hard and difficult to move from bad to good. A building may take months and years to build. But when it is done, within seconds we can drop it down and destroy it completely.

When someone says you are great and then another person says you are crap, it takes seventy seven times of saying you are great to neutralize the bad word of you are crap. Words got power and the negative ones seem to gain more input in people's lives than the positive ones. Wake up, saying to myself. You are more than a conqueror.

Get your acts together and live a straight life. Because one day when you older you will regret forever. So many people wished me bad for years. Many of them even wished to see me in the coffin or buried alive.

People that I did them well but still wanted to see me do badly. Some tried to poison me, really. No matter if you are good or bad, still people will hate you. It is not about rich or poor, the hate will be there.

Some people were born to love and others to hate. On the road to perdition, many look glad although knowing where they are heading to. It takes a real man to inspire a generation. It takes a real woman to shape the family.

A real man is not the strongest one full of muscles or the one full of money. But a real man is the one who take care of his responsibilities and give examples to others. A man can impress you with the world. A man can do whatever you want him to do.

A man can even play the role of your guardian Angel. But it is God and only Him who can lead you and give you the best feeling of this life. As I walked through my unwanted darkness, I stumbled and stumbled. Life is a test, but at that time I didn't know better.

Yet the light of God kept on shining deeper in me although I ignored it. Nothing just happens in life and some of us still very far away from us. I hung around many lonely people that late I began to be lonely too. A Weird feeling and I could even hear people talking to me loud.

Trapped in the prison of isolation, spiritually my soul and body were fighting against my spirit. Psychologically one begins to say he is cracked out, but it was the war between Good versus evil within me. The unseen is much more real than the seen. Matter of fact the Seen is a result of then unseen.

People just believe what they see and still trip when they dream about things that later happen in their lives. Some people are really crazy and more complicated than the word complication. We don't die when we get older. We don't die when we are wrong and disappear.

We don't die because of sickness and problems. But we die when we are isolated and forgotten by the others. When you can't rescue yourself, don't be shy to yell out for help. When the possible seems impossible, don't give up at all.

If people laugh at you, let them laugh but keep going where you go. Many of us die because they are afraid or shy of crying out loud. I was shy, I was afraid to compromise myself. Even though I knew the power of the Lord within me, still I couldn't use it directly.

I've been fooling myself in the madness and sadness that is more powerful than a Tornado or Volcano. Horribly my physical began failing and corresponding to the devotion of the insanity. For every one step forward, I took two steps back. If a laugh for a while, I knew already that sooner I'd cry and heavily.

The luxury of at least enjoying the air that I breathe was taken too. Yes, pretty much like a dead man walking if not worst. Any conversation of positivity automatically was shot down. If people began to talk about greatness, then I had to move myself away.

I was a fugitive in my own life and environment. Even the sweetness of sex could no longer be enjoyed at all. What a life, what a waste. What a man, what a world.

A man with no vision is no man. And a man with a vision who can not get the vision out is the worst man of all. Hours went by, days went by. Months went by and years went by.

Every New Year, the same old story happened with no glory. It was a lifestyle well known as culture of the losers. You don't go up and you don't go down. You don't go forward and you don't go backwards.

You don't move from side to side but remain in the same place. It's neutral and you are neutralized by this kind of magic so called life. I was attracted by the worst programs from the television. Just crap showing and you enjoying it.

I've been distracted by the sounds of the crazy ones who make no senses. I was the champion that was living the life with a notion of failure. Spirit of a god, soul of a giant, heart of a lion but lost in his own mind. Carrying the blood of "JESUS", body of a soldier, intelligence of a king and still not overcoming the war.

A friend in deed, reliable when you need, ready to succeed but couldn't proceed. The devil comes in many ways and if you don't resist him, he will reside in you forever. As everybody would go to sleep at night, I would be awake and just look in my window. Nights were nightmare and when I couldn't sleep I would be awake until in the morning.

At day light would sleep, but still dream about hell like is happening in reality. As you sleep, your soul would burn and you would feel it and wake up every three hours sweating like you had been doing sports. Dreams were reality and reality was hell. They are both bad choices to make when you tired of life.

You want to die but you can't die because something holds you when you confront it. And that is the Love of God backing you up and fighting with you the war against yourself. People really love to hate themselves. Saying to themselves in the mirror: I DON'T LIKE YOU: everybody is Unique and special in his or her own way.

Society loves to break us down by discerning us mentally and physically. They manipulate us and then blame us. First they give us jobs and then they rob us naked. They give us twenty percent and take from us one hundred percent.

And when we ask questions they say we want to rebel ourselves against them. The same old tricks ever since the beginning of age. The strongest dominates the weakest and the weakest accepts it. They make rules for us to obey and prohibit us from doing what is right.

When we violate their rule, it is a crime but when they violate their own rule then it is normal. The truth hurts and it is so cruel. Some of us can't deal with it and just kill themselves. Rather be dead and happy then alive and suffer forever.

When you are lost in yourself, the only one who can redeem you and gain you from yourself is yourself. Nobody will help you unless you help yourself. Before God helps you, you have to help yourself and then He will help you. If you don't respect yourself and value yourself nobody will do it for you.

It is all in our mind set where it begins and ends up. In this world we all are born with a clean heart and soul. Our spirit drives us to the loveliest things of life and attracts the attention of all. As we grow and grow, we start to see what kind of world we are into.

Suddenly it's too late and we are trapped in the ugliest and meanest place we have ever imagined. The labyrinth of destruction where many are caught and only few are saved. The labyrinth of shinny things that hypnotize our eyes and hearts then leaves us dead in the end. The labyrinth of pleasure that adores our bodies and then burn our souls. So many labyrinths, each stronger than the other but they are all curse.

Sometimes is better not to have and be just like that. When you have, then they will come to you until you don't have anything. People don't listen, especially stubborn. You may not care now, but someday you will care and feel the pressure of everything you did in your life.

Coming with peace, but facing the opposite. I've been misunderstood by the color of my skin and religious belief. I was born with love but people hated me and forced me to hate others too. No, not me and I don't want to be a part of this system any more.

Finally I found peace of mind; yes I got peace of mind. All this years, my God never left me alone and He was always there with me as my good friend in me. I won the war against the enemy within me and defeated him to a certain point where he can never take advantage of me again. The biggest enemy of our lives is not the devil or money, but we.

We are our blessings and curse. We are our good and evil. We are our victory and downfall. We, ourselves are the trouble makers and solution bringers to our own problems.

God have nothing to do with our issues. He can help us if we let Him do it for us, but it lays on us. God created it all and gave us the dominion over everything. Some of us grabbed it and now play with the rest of us.

It was never God's intention to see us suffering. It was never His will to have us in such a mess. I used to blame God for the mess people did to me. He made me understand life and gave me the solution for my problems.

The solution lays in all of us. We all got the spiritual powers inside of us and waiting to be activated. Everything that you see and feel is temporary. And everything that you envision is eternal and true.

Poverty rate increases every year. The world is full of resources but we still starve. Even great nations got poor people around them. How can it be?

A government is responsible for a certain place. If that place goes down, then that government carries the blame. In our lifetime the governments enjoy seeing people starving. I think it would be better if God could have come and erased the whole earth as he has done before and start something new.

I live free from any bad thing because I learnt the principals of overcoming. Some want to do well, but most want to do evil. Renew your mind set by speaking and practicing positive things. It is hard in the beginning but when you stick with it you will force the negative to run away from your life.

They say practice makes perfect, well nothing is perfect. But the more you practice you will get better and better improving your abilities. As long as you are ready and steady, this is it. Then nothing can intimidate you or make fool of you.

I laugh more and have more fun than ever. Physically and spiritually I'm ready for any challenge that comes ahead. I made God my Security, my one and only Source. Nothing can stop me now because I'm on the right side of life.

Back then if I could laugh, I knew for sure later I would cry. Now I can cry because I know for sure that I will laugh with heavy laughter. I'm living the real life and enjoying the enjoyable. Anything can happen and I will always sleep in peace like a baby with no worries.

I never have been this happy before. I call myself the happiest man alive. I'm not the richest man alive or the strongest man alive. But I'm the most blessed man alive with a divine spirit, clean soul, clear mind and healthy body.

Mama is the happiest woman alive. I forgave daddy and I love him from far. I got children of my own and they are all in good spirit. I'm doing what God blessed me to do with my life.

Releasing all my talents and letting the world enjoy them. Helping others where I can and keeping the good spirit. I Speak blessings because I'm around blessings. I am a living example to my generation and ready to impact the next generation.

I was once the lost child now I am the found child. I've been driven to the darkest places of this universe and overcame the challenges of my life. If I could do it, believe me you too can do it. Anybody willing to change and to be great can achieve it by confronting the challenges of life.

Mama always said never is to early or too late to start something. If you can't do it on your own, ask God for guidance. People always disappoint you, so learn how to trust the Lord. He can and he will give you more than you ever imagine.

A new expensive car can crash badly. But when they take it to the manufactures they will make it brand new and ready for the road again. With God is even much greater than anything else. He can make us prosperous and victorious to a certain point that whatever we do, will be blessings in people's lives.

Money is good when used in a good way, but when is used badly then it's evil. Control your money and don't be controlled by it. It is not bad to have money as long as it is good money. Because bad money carries souls of people and brings bad luck.

Tribulations come and go, but a clean spirit deals with it silently. When you are on the right path, you will feel like I feel now: PEACEFUL. I made peace with God; I made peace with myself and my closest Family. Things that used to bother me, don't border me anymore because I found my way out.

I didn't do it by myself, but the most work I did myself. It is worthy, every little bit of it is heavenly. I see things differently now as I saw back then. I can't say nothing but be happy and live life to the fullest.

Everything we have on earth is the result of our thinking or thoughts. Before things happen we must call or envision them in our minds. Whether good or bad it comes from the inside to the outside of us. That's why our tongues carry the power of life and death to us.

If we all go back to Mother Nature and understand her, we will understand life and live happily. The connection between Nature and us is the Essential point for our lives. We need and we must know that freedom with no wisdom is like a body with no Soul. The challenges of life are not just there to destroy us but to strengthen us and give us experiences in order to overcome obstacles and live happy.

There is a disease more dangerous than Aids, Cancer or Heart attack. It kills more people than Cigarettes do, matter of fact it is the cause that leads people to smoke a lot. It is called "STRESS" and burns your brain by killing you mentally. Stress leads to depression and a depressed human being doesn't care or fear anything in the world.

The Government through all its ways gives us stress in order to kill us mentally and physically. It is not a new thing but only few people know the truth and some don't even want to acknowledge that. To be a live means to live in abundance in all areas of one's life. But today in our lives we burn ourselves for the sake of money and good things that don't even make us happy.

As we come on earth, we come full and must leave empty. Some of us come full and unfortunately leave full. It's a tragedy when you cannot use nor do your homework as you were assigned to do on earth by God. Just like the Biblical story about the Master and his three servants which he gave them talents to produce more talents.

One he gave five talents, the other two talents and the third he gave one talent. He went away telling them he would come back home after a period of time. The one with five talents produced five more talents, the one with two talents produced two more talents and the third one has produced nothing. And when the Master has returned home, he blessed those two who reproduce their talents and cursed the one who reproduced nothing.

The point is we must be what we are destined to be. By releasing our gifts from inside to the world we sow our seeds and everyone loves to reap what he sows. Don't hate the success of others because you don't know what they had been through to get it. If we don't change our mindset than we will never change the way we act and live.

Love me as I am or leave me alone. I rather please myself than please others in order to gain their recognition. No one is perfect and I need no perfection to have a happy home. As long as we respect and treat each other fairly then the love will guide us to a wonderful life.

The urgency of knowledge and self-confidence is needed in our lives. If we know who we are and understand why we are here, then nobody will be able to manipulate us as they have been doing. As Human beings, we all are great ones with the potential to have anything we want or need. We are the Goods and Evils to ourselves and hold the final decision to our Victory or Downfall.

To know, to understand and to accept the real you it frees you from all the false evidence portrayed by this world of your real you. We are more than we think we are and within us we carry spiritual treasuries that one could never imagine. They don't want us to discover ourselves and stress us so that we lose the vision of who we really are. I've discovered who I really am by force and I'm proud to have fought the war within me.

For the first time in my life I can say proudly: ANYTHING IS POSSIBLE WHEN YOU BELIEVE. The enemy within me is gone, yes he is gone forever. I thank God for everything that he did in my life even when I didn't see it was God helping me out. We are all winners and we can overcome whatever challenges of life.

As human beings, we are more equals than many think. We share many common things that only few realize. I'm going through the whole world spreading my victory as examples for others who are still captives in their own minds. I defeated the enemy within me, what about you?

Written by: GASPAR ANDRADE:

GASPAR ANDRADE

Am Südhang 15

57072-Siegen

Germany

Tel: 004917668680073

www.ingramcontent.com/pod-product-compliance
Lightning Source LLC
Chambersburg PA
CBHW021252280526
45784CB00005B/2348